T0021668

LAW OF
ATTRACTION
MANIFESTATION
JOURNAL

LAW OF ATTRACTION MANIFESTATION JOURNAL

A GUIDED JOURNAL FOR MANIFESTING YOUR DEEPEST DESIRES

LATHA JAY

ZEITGEIST · NEW YORK

Copyright © 2022 by Penguin Random House LLC
All rights reserved.

Published in the United States by Zeitgeist, an imprint of Zeitgeist™,
a division of Penguin Random House LLC, New York.
penguinrandomhouse.com

Zeitgeist™ is a trademark of Penguin Random House LLC

ISBN: 9780593435564

Cover and interior art © by Arelix/Shutterstock.com,
Artnis/Shutterstock.com, and maybealice/Shutterstock.com
Author photo © by Jessica Danae Photography

Cover design by Katy Brown
Interior design by Aimee Fleck

Printed in the United States of America

3 5 7 9 10 8 6 4 2

First Edition

Contents

Introduction

Manifestation is part of my family heritage. At a very young age, I learned how to manifest from my grandmother, Valliammal, who lived most of her life in Tamil Nadu, India. Although her family was very poor, she recalled to me that they always had their thoughts, and with them, they could create anything. She eventually manifested her way from living in a home with a dirt floor as one of ten children to enjoying the luxuries of life in America.

One summer, I went with her to India to visit family. This was where I first observed her, with pure shock and delight, manifesting things like getting us into a sold-out event or calling a certain item or food into existence. Later, she would tell me how she would bring the thought to her mind and add in emotion to bring it to fruition. She even showed me the journals upon journals in which she scripted her future.

When I was in first grade, we were having a Mother's Day raffle, and I really wanted to win the little floral-printed vase for my grandmother. That night, I went home and wrote, "I got the vase." As I did this, I also thought about how happy my grandmother was to get the gift and how this gesture let her know how much I cared about her. The next day, I won the raffle. My classmate Stephanie asked me, "How did you do that?" to which I matter-of-factly replied, "I just thought about it with my heart." Stephanie gave me a strange look, and we dropped the subject.

Over the next few years, it became obvious to me that manifesting wasn't something everybody knew about, and it definitely wasn't something everybody did. This perplexed me. Why wouldn't people want to manifest? Why wouldn't they want to consciously create? And then it dawned on me: They did not know how.

As a child, my first few attempts to explain manifesting didn't go over so well. I'd fumble through the Tamil-to-English translations and didn't have all the right words to get the meaning across. Because of this, I started to shy away from sharing what I knew. It wasn't until I was in my late teens and read *The Secret* by Rhonda Byrne that I realized a lot of people did know about manifesting, and it was confirmation that anyone could learn to do it.

Today, I enjoy teaching people how to manifest because I love the excitement and understanding they experience when it clicks for them. For some people, this "aha" moment happens when they discover the root cause of a limiting belief. When they shine a light on this shadow, it loses its power over them. This is the beginning of healing and shifting one's mindset: They now have a sense of ownership over their lives that empowers them in a way they have never experienced before. This can be true for you, too.

VALLIAMMAL AND LATHA
NEW YORK, JUNE 2017

MANIFESTING WITH THE LAW OF ATTRACTION

Manifestation is the process of creating what you want in your life through your thoughts, beliefs, and actions. Whether you are consciously aware of it or not, you are manifesting. If you are unaware of this ability, you are subconsciously creating by default. This gives your limiting beliefs and doubts the power of creation. However, when you are consciously manifesting, YOU have the power to create your life as you want it to be.

When you are consciously manifesting, you are attuning yourself to the things you want in your life and the goals you desire to reach. When you add emotion, thought, and aligned action to this attunement, you start taking steps to make your desires a reality. As you move forward with faith, you see your desires start to materialize.

The Law of Attraction is the ability to attract things, people, and situations into your life by using focused thought and emotion. It is the concept that whatever you put your attention on grows and whatever you imagine and hold to be true in your mind you create in your life. In short, it is the ability to manifest thoughts into reality. Because everything starts out as a thought, before anything can become real, you must first think it. In this way, positive thoughts bring about positive experiences and negative thoughts bring about negative experiences.

Key Principles

Where our focus goes, grows. Whatever you dedicate your energy to is inevitably going to grow. When you focus your attention on positive things, you cultivate more positivity.

Like attracts like. We can only attract into our lives what we are. When you ground yourself in actions of love and positivity, you begin to cultivate and attract love and positivity in return.

What we put out we get back. Energy is like a boomerang. The more energy you put into throwing the boomerang, the more energy it will bring back to you when it returns. When you put out good energy into the world, that is what you will receive.

Life is a mirror. The energy we feel within us is the world we create around us. The feelings and emotions you have within you create the world around you, which is why it is important to shed light on your limiting beliefs, those negative thoughts that hold you back.

Writing Your Destiny

Writing down what you desire is a crucial part of manifesting because the act of writing itself is an act of creation. Writing takes the thought, desire, or idea out of the ether space of your mind and brings it one step closer to reality because it now exists on paper. Here are a few powerful manifestation methods that involve writing:

The 369 Method. This method guides you to write down what you wish to manifest three times in the morning, six times in the afternoon, and nine times in the evening. This is done for several days, ideally with a routine in place, repeating morning, afternoon, and evening writings around the same times each day.

This technique highlights the numbers three, six, and nine, which are believed to be divine. The number three reflects our connection to the universe, the number six reflects our own strength, and the number nine reflects our transformation and ability to let go of what is no longer serving us to make room for what will.

The 55x5 Method. This method assists you in aligning yourself with what you want to manifest. It utilizes repetition and commitment to work directly with your subconscious and show the universe that you are ready to receive your manifestation. In numerology, the number five represents transformation; therefore, the number 555 represents great transformation.

This technique involves choosing an affirmation and writing it down fifty-five times per day for five consecutive days. This is not just rote repetition. Rather, it is done with purpose so that you can feel the emotions behind the words and truly connect to their meaning. As you write the affirmation, visualize what you wish to manifest as if it is already yours and feel the feelings of already having it.

The Scripting Method. In scripting, you write out your life as you want it to be in the present tense using positive words from the perspective of your future self. Scripting is like the sister of visualization, and it is ideal for folks who might struggle with making their visualizations detailed and vivid. When you script, you are encouraged to include as much detail as possible about how it feels and looks to have what you desire.

Secrets to Success

Get clear on what you want. Clarity is key. The first step to manifesting anything is to get clear on what you want. Think of it like this: The universe is a restaurant. If you walk into this restaurant and ask for "food," you might get a slice of pizza, a salad, a meat loaf, and so on. You could then become upset when you don't get the burger you really wanted. Had you been clear and asked for "a burger," you would have received a burger. This is your life—ask specifically for the burger.

Deal with your limiting beliefs. The only things holding you back from manifesting are your limiting beliefs. Just as you can create anything you want, you can also create limitations. When you have a limiting belief, it sets an unhealthy boundary around what you are able to create and accomplish. However, when you deal with your limiting beliefs through therapy, shadow work, or other methods of self-exploration, you can grow free and boundless in your ability to manifest.

Use affirmations. Affirmations come in two forms. One is a short "I am" statement that can help you rewrite some of your current limiting beliefs. For example, if a limiting belief is, "I am unlovable and not good enough," a positive "I am" statement rewrite would be, "I am lovable. I am enough."

The second type of affirmation is a positive statement in the present tense regarding what you are manifesting. This type of affirmation brings your desire into the now and links it with emotion. For example, if your desired manifestation is a romantic relationship, your manifestation affirmation could be, "I am happy and grateful now that I am in a loving relationship."

Channel positive emotions to boost your manifestation. Although you can manifest with any emotion, love, joy, and gratitude are some of the most powerful emotions to use. Make every effort to be in these emotional states while working on your manifestation.

Visualize as if you already have it. See yourself having what you desire to manifest, not as if you are watching a movie of yourself having your desire, but as if you are in the movie. For example, if you are looking to manifest a new car, see your hand opening the car door as you climb into your brand-new car.

Work in alignment with nature. Although you can manifest at any time, you can supercharge your manifestations by aligning them with the rhythm of the lunar cycle. The new moon, which symbolizes new beginnings, has a powerful energy for welcoming or bringing new things into your life. The full moon, symbolizing completion and closure, is the perfect time to release what is no longer serving you. Just as we breathe in, we must breathe out to make space for the next nursing breath in.

Take aligned action. Be in alignment with what you want to manifest by taking some steps toward your desired goal. If you do the written manifestation steps consistently and passionately but don't take actions that bring you closer to your desire, nothing will come of it. Let your actions signal to the universe that you're ready.

How to Use This Journal

What's the best method to manifest with? The one that works! Because we all have different routines, thoughts, ideas, and limiting beliefs, manifesting is a very individualized process. These factors, along with countless others, impact which method will work best for you. Try all three methods outlined and continue using the one that resonates with you the most.

Before you sit down with this journal, get into a relaxed state. You may want to pour yourself a nice cup of tea and pick up your favorite pen, or maybe roll on some lavender essential oil and sit somewhere comfy. If you have a few minutes, try to center yourself or meditate with this journal nearby. Once you feel that you're in true stillness, open your journal and begin.

CRAFTING AFFIRMATIONS FOR MANIFESTATION

A central part of manifesting is crafting strong affirmations that clearly and effectively communicate your desires to the universe. Thus, when creating the affirmations for your writing manifestations, remember the following guidelines:

1. Be specific. Vague affirmations run the risk of creating messy or unintended interpretations.

2. Infuse your statement with positive emotions like love, gratitude, or joy. These emotions emit higher vibrations to the universe, which result in more favorable outcomes.

3. Use positive language in the present tense, writing as if the intended manifestation were already true. Doing so helps to develop trust in your inner knowing, creating a confidence that's critical for manifesting.

For example, if you want to manifest more money, you can write, "I am so happy and grateful now that I have an additional five hundred dollars." Note that it's not enough to say, "I'm so happy I have more money" because "more money" can mean anything, and technically even an extra dollar would fulfill your manifestation.

CHAPTER 2

THREE POWERFUL MANIFESTATION METHODS

The 369 Method

Well-known engineer Nikola Tesla believed that multiples of three could harness the power of the universe and unlock its secrets using energy, frequency, and vibration. This method uses the 3-6-9 number sequence to help amplify your manifestation abilities.

When using this method, it is imperative to feel the feelings of your manifestation as if it is already a reality and visualize it as if it is already true. It is not enough to write down your affirmations like a robot. The power of manifesting is in your emotions and visualizations. That's the secret sauce. Here's how:

1. Check in with yourself and what you want to manifest. Remember to be clear and specific about what you want.

2. Create a positive affirmation with one or two sentences in the present tense.

3. As soon as you wake up in the morning, grab this journal and write down your affirmation three times. The most powerful time to do this is immediately upon waking—before you brush your teeth, before you have your morning brew, and even before your feet touch the ground.

4. In the afternoon, open this journal and write down your affirmation six times.

5. As you are cozying up to go to sleep, pick up this journal and write your affirmation nine times. This journal and your pen should be the last things you touch (other than your light) before you close your eyes.

Each time you write your affirmation, remember to feel the feelings of already having what you want to manifest.

The reason for writing immediately upon awakening and right before you fall asleep is because these are the most powerful times to manifest. This period between sleep and wakefulness is called a hypnagogic state. This is when your subconscious is the most impressionable.

Setting an alarm can help get you into the routine and serve as a reminder for you to write three times a day. The reminder will be especially helpful for the afternoon session.

Repeat this daily routine for at least thirty-three days or until your manifestation comes to fruition. Stay committed and consistent. If you ever feel that it is becoming a chore, remind yourself of how much you truly want this. Some people may see results around twenty-one days, and some people may need longer. It varies from person to person, and the length of time it takes depends on your belief in this manifestation becoming a reality.

What matters is your energy and the energy you put behind the actions you take to get closer to your goal. Make sure you are matching the emotional frequency of what you are manifesting. Stay in a high-vibrational place with feelings of love, joy, gratitude, and patience. When something is high vibrational, you have a sense of ease around it. Things feel lighter. High-vibrational energy can be felt when bringing up positive emotions. On the other hand, when something is low vibrational, it feels heavy. Low-vibrational energy can be felt around the emotions of stress, sadness, and anxiety. Becoming ungrateful, agitated, or pushy about your manifestation coming true is low-vibrational energy, which does the opposite of what you want to do.

Follow divine inspiration and be in aligned action. When you see an unusual or exciting opportunity open up, take it. Focusing on your desires on a consistent basis will keep you on track to achieve your goal. However, keep in mind that being focused on your manifestation (that is, working toward a goal) is different from being obsessed, consumed, or overwhelmed by achieving an outcome. These are very low-vibrational energies and not the space you want to be creating from.

The 55x5 Method

This method shifts your mindset at a subconscious level. It creates a structure for you to bring your manifestation to fruition. It is ideal for people who have difficulty being consistent and need a little bit more structure in their technique. Over the course of five consecutive days, you will consistently align yourself with your desire using concentrated energy.

The 55x5 method works because it assists you in focusing on your intention, allows for repetition, and creates commitment. The number five is significant in numerology as it is the number that represents transformation. It's the number that's often associated with growth, change, and transition. The transformation associated with the number five is thought to bring you closer to your life's purpose. Here's how to do it:

1. Check in with yourself and what you want to manifest. Remember to be clear and specific about what you want.

2. Write a positive affirmation in the present tense. Keep it short: one sentence max. Remember to be specific and lean into the emotions that resonate with you from the words you choose.

3. Get comfy in a calm space and write your affirmation fifty-five times.

4. Repeat steps 1–3 for the remaining four days.

As you are writing your affirmation, feel the feelings as though what you want is already yours. Visualize your life as if this affirmation is a reality. Stick with it. There is power in the commitment and consistency. If you miss a day, start over again from day one. Remember, this is a joyous practice. This is not something to become overwhelmed by or to rush.

Choose a time of day when you generally feel most at peace and can journal uninterrupted. It's highly recommended that you take a few minutes to sit in stillness and meditate before writing your fifty-five repetitions. For most people, the writing process will take thirty to sixty minutes. Make sure to set aside adequate time to focus on what you are creating. Schedule it in your calendar, set an alarm for it, show up, and make it happen!

The Scripting Method

Scripting is the art of reimagining your life in an intentional way, in the form of a written story. This method harnesses the power of the Law of Attraction by guiding you to write what you wish to manifest as if you're reflecting or reminiscing on what already is. This is you literally writing the next chapter of your life. Scripting can shift your reality as you begin to believe what you are creating through writing.

This is a powerful method of manifesting because it allows for a lot of freedom, creativity, and play. It gives your imagination space to expand upon your desires and access your emotions and multiple areas of thought. It isn't limited to just one area of your life. Here's how to do it:

1. Have an idea of what it is you want your future to look like. This method does not require you to be concise.

2. From the perspective of your future self, write in the present tense using positive words. Even though you are writing what your future will look like, write as if it is already your reality.

3. Be detailed. The details connect you with what you want and invoke emotions that align with your desire. How does it look,

feel, smell, sound, taste? Who else is present? Where are you? What are you doing? What are you surrounded by?

4.   Include your feelings in your script. Describe how you feel having these things and being this future version of yourself. Express yourself and your emotions fully, including your gratitude for what you have created.

5.   Believe it. To create this future version of yourself, you must believe in it. Believe you are capable of having it.

Set aside fifteen to twenty minutes daily to do this. You don't have to write the whole time. Take some time to visualize what your future self is like. Use some of this time to conjure up the emotions of what it feels like to be this fabulous future version of you. You can script for the week ahead, six months ahead, or even ten years down the line. The version of your future self is completely up to you!

There's no structured time requirement for how many days you should script. Follow your intuition on this one. Keep going, keep writing, and keep creating. Remember to let go of any attachment to an outcome. When we are attached to an outcome we become hyper-focused and fixated on something happening. In that fixation we lose joy. We allow the attachment to drain our faith in our own ability to make something happen. When we are attached we are shackled and often trying to force an outcome to happen in a certain way. Being attached to an outcome comes from a place of lack, desperation, and need. This is not where you want your energy to go while manifesting.

Scripting Prompts to Help You Get Started

Scripting for a romantic relationship. How do you feel in this relationship? What do you and your partner do on date night? Do you prefer to go out or stay in? What hobbies do you enjoy doing together? What characteristics about your partner do you appreciate the most? Which of their physical features do you like best? How does your partner dress? How does your partner treat you?

Scripting for a new car. What is the make, model, and year of the car? What color is the car? How does it feel when you are sitting in the driver's seat? How does the steering wheel feel under your hands? How does the car smell? What does the dashboard look like?

Scripting for a new home. Where is your home located? How many bathrooms and bedrooms does it have? What's the style of your home? How have you furnished it? What's the backyard like? What are your home's notable features? Every time you walk through your front door, what does it give you a sense of? Visualize having a dinner party and inviting your favorite people over for a meal in your new dining room; describe it.

Scripting for money. How much money do you want to manifest? What are you doing with the money? How does having this amount of money make you feel? What are you able to purchase with this money? How do you share this wealth with others?

CHAPTER 3

YOUR

369

MANIFESTATION SPACE

Date:

Your Desired Manifestation:

_____

_____

TIME: _____ : _____ AM / PM

1. _____

2. _____

3. _____

TIME: _____ : _____ AM / PM

1. _____

2. _____

3. _____

4. _____

5. _____

6. _____

TIME: _____ : _____ AM / PM

1. _____

2. _____

3. _____

4. _____

5. _____

6. _____

7. _____

8. _____

9. _____

Date:

Your Desired Manifestation:

_____

_____

TIME: _____ : _____ AM / PM

1 . _____

2 . _____

3 . _____

TIME: _____ : _____ AM / PM

1 . _____

2 . _____

3 . _____

4 . _____

5 . _____

6 . _____

TIME: _____ : _____ AM / PM

1 . _____

2 . _____

3 . _____

4 . _____

5 . _____

6 . _____

7 . _____

8 . _____

9 . _____

Date:

Your Desired Manifestation:

TIME: ___ : ___ AM / PM

1 .

2 .

3 .

TIME: ___ : ___ AM / PM

1 .

2 .

3 .

4 .

5 .

6 .

TIME: ___ : ___ AM / PM

1 .

2 .

3 .

4 .

5 .

6 .

7 .

8 .

9 .

Date:

Your Desired Manifestation:

_____

_____

TIME: _____ : _____ AM / PM

1. _____

2. _____

3. _____

TIME: _____ : _____ AM / PM

1. _____

2. _____

3. _____

4. _____

5. _____

6. _____

TIME: _____ : _____ AM / PM

1. _____

2. _____

3. _____

4. _____

5. _____

6. _____

7. _____

8. _____

9. _____

Date:

Your Desired Manifestation:

TIME: _____ : _____ AM / PM

1 .

2 .

3 .

TIME: _____ : _____ AM / PM

1 .

2 .

3 .

4 .

5 .

6 .

TIME: _____ : _____ AM / PM

1 .

2 .

3 .

4 .

5 .

6 .

7 .

8 .

9 .

Date:

Your Desired Manifestation:

TIME: _____ : _____ AM / PM

1 .

2 .

3 .

TIME: _____ : _____ AM / PM

1 .

2 .

3 .

4 .

5 .

6 .

TIME: _____ : _____ AM / PM

1 .

2 .

3 .

4 .

5 .

6 .

7 .

8 .

9 .

Date: | **Your Desired Manifestation:**

TIME: _____ : _____ AM / PM

1 .

2 .

3 .

TIME: _____ : _____ AM / PM

1 .

2 .

3 .

4 .

5 .

6 .

TIME: _____ : _____ AM / PM

1 .

2 .

3 .

4 .

5 .

6 .

7 .

8 .

9 .

Date:

Your Desired Manifestation:

TIME: _____ : _____ AM / PM

1. _____
2. _____
3. _____

TIME: _____ : _____ AM / PM

1. _____
2. _____
3. _____
4. _____
5. _____
6. _____

TIME: _____ : _____ AM / PM

1. _____
2. _____
3. _____
4. _____
5. _____
6. _____
7. _____
8. _____
9. _____

Date:

Your Desired Manifestation:

....

....

TIME: _____ : _____ AM / PM

1 . ...

2 . ...

3 . ...

TIME: _____ : _____ AM / PM

1 . ...

2 . ...

3 . ...

4 . ...

5 . ...

6 . ...

TIME: _____ : _____ AM / PM

1 . ...

2 . ...

3 . ...

4 . ...

5 . ...

6 . ...

7 . ...

8 . ...

9 . ...

Date:

Your Desired Manifestation:

TIME: _____ : _____ AM / PM

1.

2.

3.

TIME: _____ : _____ AM / PM

1.

2.

3.

4.

5.

6.

TIME: _____ : _____ AM / PM

1.

2.

3.

4.

5.

6.

7.

8.

9.

Date:

Your Desired Manifestation:

TIME: _____ : _____ AM / PM

1 .

2 .

3 .

TIME: _____ : _____ AM / PM

1 .

2 .

3 .

4 .

5 .

6 .

TIME: _____ : _____ AM / PM

1 .

2 .

3 .

4 .

5 .

6 .

7 .

8 .

9 .

Date:

Your Desired Manifestation:

TIME: _____ : _____ AM / PM

1 .

2 .

3 .

TIME: _____ : _____ AM / PM

1 .

2 .

3 .

4 .

5 .

6 .

TIME: _____ : _____ AM / PM

1 .

2 .

3 .

4 .

5 .

6 .

7 .

8 .

9 .

Date:

Your Desired Manifestation:

TIME: ___ ___ : ___ ___ AM / PM

1.
2.
3.

TIME: ___ ___ : ___ ___ AM / PM

1.
2.
3.
4.
5.
6.

TIME: ___ ___ : ___ ___ AM / PM

1.
2.
3.
4.
5.
6.
7.
8.
9.

Date:

Your Desired Manifestation:

TIME: _____ : _____ AM / PM

1 .

2 .

3 .

TIME: _____ : _____ AM / PM

1 .

2 .

3 .

4 .

5 .

6 .

TIME: _____ : _____ AM / PM

1 .

2 .

3 .

4 .

5 .

6 .

7 .

8 .

9 .

Date:

Your Desired Manifestation:

TIME: ___ : ___ AM / PM

1 .

2 .

3 .

TIME: ___ : ___ AM / PM

1 .

2 .

3 .

4 .

5 .

6 .

TIME: ___ : ___ AM / PM

1 .

2 .

3 .

4 .

5 .

6 .

7 .

8 .

9 .

Date:

Your Desired Manifestation:

TIME: _____ : _____ AM / PM

1.

2.

3.

TIME: _____ : _____ AM / PM

1.

2.

3.

4.

5.

6.

TIME: _____ : _____ AM / PM

1.

2.

3.

4.

5.

6.

7.

8.

9.

Date:

Your Desired Manifestation:

_____

_____

TIME: _____ : _____ AM / PM

1 . _____

2 . _____

3 . _____

TIME: _____ : _____ AM / PM

1 . _____

2 . _____

3 . _____

4 . _____

5 . _____

6 . _____

TIME: _____ : _____ AM / PM

1 . _____

2 . _____

3 . _____

4 . _____

5 . _____

6 . _____

7 . _____

8 . _____

9 . _____

Date:

Your Desired Manifestation:

_____

_____

TIME: _____ : _____ AM / PM

1. _____
2. _____
3. _____

TIME: _____ : _____ AM / PM

1. _____
2. _____
3. _____
4. _____
5. _____
6. _____

TIME: _____ : _____ AM / PM

1. _____
2. _____
3. _____
4. _____
5. _____
6. _____
7. _____
8. _____
9. _____

Date:

Your Desired Manifestation:

_____

_____

TIME: ____ : ____ AM / PM

1. _____
2. _____
3. _____

TIME: ____ : ____ AM / PM

1. _____
2. _____
3. _____
4. _____
5. _____
6. _____

TIME: ____ : ____ AM / PM

1. _____
2. _____
3. _____
4. _____
5. _____
6. _____
7. _____
8. _____
9. _____

Date: | **Your Desired Manifestation:**

TIME: _____ : _____ AM / PM

1 .

2 .

3 .

TIME: _____ : _____ AM / PM

1 .

2 .

3 .

4 .

5 .

6 .

TIME: _____ : _____ AM / PM

1 .

2 .

3 .

4 .

5 .

6 .

7 .

8 .

9 .

Date:

Your Desired Manifestation:

TIME: _____ : _____ AM / PM

1 .

2 .

3 .

TIME: _____ : _____ AM / PM

1 .

2 .

3 .

4 .

5 .

6 .

TIME: _____ : _____ AM / PM

1 .

2 .

3 .

4 .

5 .

6 .

7 .

8 .

9 .

Date:

Your Desired Manifestation:

TIME: ____ : ____ AM / PM

1 .

2 .

3 .

TIME: ____ : ____ AM / PM

1 .

2 .

3 .

4 .

5 .

6 .

TIME: ____ : ____ AM / PM

1 .

2 .

3 .

4 .

5 .

6 .

7 .

8 .

9 .

Date:

Your Desired Manifestation:

TIME: _____ : _____ AM / PM

1 .

2 .

3 .

TIME: _____ : _____ AM / PM

1 .

2 .

3 .

4 .

5 .

6 .

TIME: _____ : _____ AM / PM

1 .

2 .

3 .

4 .

5 .

6 .

7 .

8 .

9 .

Date:

Your Desired Manifestation:

_____

_____

TIME: _____ : _____ AM / PM

1. _____
2. _____
3. _____

TIME: _____ : _____ AM / PM

1. _____
2. _____
3. _____
4. _____
5. _____
6. _____

TIME: _____ : _____ AM / PM

1. _____
2. _____
3. _____
4. _____
5. _____
6. _____
7. _____
8. _____
9. _____

Date:

Your Desired Manifestation:

TIME: _____ : _____ AM / PM

1 .

2 .

3 .

TIME: _____ : _____ AM / PM

1 .

2 .

3 .

4 .

5 .

6 .

TIME: _____ : _____ AM / PM

1 .

2 .

3 .

4 .

5 .

6 .

7 .

8 .

9 .

Date:

Your Desired Manifestation:

TIME: _____ : _____ AM / PM

1 .

2 .

3 .

TIME: _____ : _____ AM / PM

1 .

2 .

3 .

4 .

5 .

6 .

TIME: _____ : _____ AM / PM

1 .

2 .

3 .

4 .

5 .

6 .

7 .

8 .

9 .

Date:

Your Desired Manifestation:

TIME: _____ : _____ AM / PM

1.
2.
3.

TIME: _____ : _____ AM / PM

1.
2.
3.
4.
5.
6.

TIME: _____ : _____ AM / PM

1.
2.
3.
4.
5.
6.
7.
8.
9.

Date: | **Your Desired Manifestation:**

_____

_____

_____

TIME: ___ ___ : ___ ___ AM / PM

1. _____

2. _____

3. _____

TIME: ___ ___ : ___ ___ AM / PM

1. _____

2. _____

3. _____

4. _____

5. _____

6. _____

TIME: ___ ___ : ___ ___ AM / PM

1. _____

2. _____

3. _____

4. _____

5. _____

6. _____

7. _____

8. _____

9. _____

Date:

Your Desired Manifestation:

_____

_____

TIME: _____ : _____ AM / PM

1 . _____

2 . _____

3 . _____

TIME: _____ : _____ AM / PM

1 . _____

2 . _____

3 . _____

4 . _____

5 . _____

6 . _____

TIME: _____ : _____ AM / PM

1 . _____

2 . _____

3 . _____

4 . _____

5 . _____

6 . _____

7 . _____

8 . _____

9 . _____

Date:

Your Desired Manifestation:

_____

_____

TIME: ____ : ____ AM / PM

1. _____
2. _____
3. _____

TIME: ____ : ____ AM / PM

1. _____
2. _____
3. _____
4. _____
5. _____
6. _____

TIME: ____ : ____ AM / PM

1. _____
2. _____
3. _____
4. _____
5. _____
6. _____
7. _____
8. _____
9. _____

Date:

Your Desired Manifestation:

TIME: _____ : _____ AM / PM

1 .

2 .

3 .

TIME: _____ : _____ AM / PM

1 .

2 .

3 .

4 .

5 .

6 .

TIME: _____ : _____ AM / PM

1 .

2 .

3 .

4 .

5 .

6 .

7 .

8 .

9 .

Date:

Your Desired Manifestation:

_____

_____

TIME: _____ : _____ AM / PM

1. _____

2. _____

3. _____

TIME: _____ : _____ AM / PM

1. _____

2. _____

3. _____

4. _____

5. _____

6. _____

TIME: _____ : _____ AM / PM

1. _____

2. _____

3. _____

4. _____

5. _____

6. _____

7. _____

8. _____

9. _____

Date:

Your Desired Manifestation:

TIME: ___ ___ : ___ ___ AM / PM

1 .

2 .

3 .

TIME: ___ ___ : ___ ___ AM / PM

1 .

2 .

3 .

4 .

5 .

6 .

TIME: ___ ___ : ___ ___ AM / PM

1 .

2 .

3 .

4 .

5 .

6 .

7 .

8 .

9 .

CHAPTER 4

YOUR

55x5

MANIFESTATION SPACE

Day: _____ of 5

Date:

Your Desired Manifestation:

1 .

2 .

3 .

4 .

5 .

6 .

7 .

8 .

9 .

10 .

11 .

12 .

13 .

14 .

15 .

16 .

17 .

18 .

19 .

20.

21 .

22 .

23 .

24 .

25 .

26 .

27 .

28 .

29 .

30.

31 .

32 .

33 .

34 .

35 .

36. _____

37. _____

38. _____

39. _____

40. _____

41. _____

42. _____

43. _____

44. _____

45. _____

46. _____

47. _____

48. _____

49. _____

50. _____

51. _____

52. _____

53. _____

54. _____

55. _____

Your 55×5 Manifestation Space

Day: _____ of 5

Date:

Your Desired Manifestation:

_____

_____

_____

1. _____
2. _____
3. _____
4. _____
5. _____
6. _____
7. _____
8. _____
9. _____
10. _____
11. _____
12. _____
13. _____
14. _____
15. _____

16.

17.

18.

19.

20.

21.

22.

23.

24.

25.

26.

27.

28.

29.

30.

31.

32.

33.

34.

35.

36.

37.

38.

39.

40.

41.

42.

43.

44.

45.

46.

47.

48.

49.

50.

51.

52.

53.

54.

55.

Day: _____ of 5

Date:

Your Desired Manifestation:

1.
2.
3.
4.
5.
6.
7.
8.
9.
10.
11.
12.
13.
14.
15.

16.

17.

18.

19.

20.

21.

22.

23.

24.

25.

26.

27.

28.

29.

30.

31.

32.

33.

34.

35.

36.

37.

38.

39.

40.

41.

42.

43.

44.

45.

46.

47.

48.

49.

50.

51.

52.

53.

54.

55.

Day: _____ of 5

Date:

Your Desired Manifestation:

_____

_____

_____

_____

1 . _____

2 . _____

3 . _____

4 . _____

5 . _____

6 . _____

7 . _____

8 . _____

9 . _____

10. _____

11. _____

12. _____

13. _____

14. _____

15. _____

16.

17.

18.

19.

20.

21.

22.

23.

24.

25.

26.

27.

28.

29.

30.

31.

32.

33.

34.

35.

36.

37.

38.

39.

40.

41.

42.

43.

44.

45.

46.

47.

48.

49.

50.

51.

52.

53.

54.

55.

Day: _____ of 5

Date:

Your Desired Manifestation:

1 .
2 .
3 .
4 .
5 .
6 .
7 .
8 .
9 .
10 .
11 .
12 .
13 .
14 .
15 .

16.

17.

18.

19.

20.

21.

22.

23.

24.

25.

26.

27.

28.

29.

30.

31.

32.

33.

34.

35.

36.

37.

38.

39.

40.

41.

42.

43.

44.

45.

46.

47.

48.

49.

50.

51.

52.

53.

54.

55.

Day: _____ of 5

Date:

Your Desired Manifestation:

1 .

2 .

3 .

4 .

5 .

6 .

7 .

8 .

9 .

10 .

11 .

12 .

13 .

14 .

15 .

16 .

17 .

18 .

19 .

20.

21 .

22 .

23 .

24 .

25 .

26 .

27 .

28 .

29 .

30.

31 .

32 .

33 .

34 .

35 .

36.

37.

38.

39.

40.

41.

42.

43.

44.

45.

46.

47.

48.

49.

50.

51.

52.

53.

54.

55.

Day: _____ of 5

Date:

Your Desired Manifestation:

1 .
2 .
3 .
4 .
5 .
6 .
7 .
8 .
9 .
10 .
11 .
12 .
13 .
14 .
15 .

16.

17.

18.

19.

20.

21.

22.

23.

24.

25.

26.

27.

28.

29.

30.

31.

32.

33.

34.

35.

36.

37.

38.

39.

40.

41.

42.

43.

44.

45.

46.

47.

48.

49.

50.

51.

52.

53.

54.

55.

Day: _____ of 5

Date:

Your Desired Manifestation:

_____
_____
_____

1. _____
2. _____
3. _____
4. _____
5. _____
6. _____
7. _____
8. _____
9. _____
10. _____
11. _____
12. _____
13. _____
14. _____
15. _____

16.

17.

18.

19.

20.

21.

22.

23.

24.

25.

26.

27.

28.

29.

30.

31.

32.

33.

34.

35.

36.

37.

38.

39.

40.

41.

42.

43.

44.

45.

46.

47.

48.

49.

50.

51.

52.

53.

54.

55.

Day: _____ of 5

Date:

Your Desired Manifestation:

1 .
2 .
3 .
4 .
5 .
6 .
7 .
8 .
9 .
10 .
11 .
12 .
13 .
14 .
15 .

16.

17.

18.

19.

20.

21.

22.

23.

24.

25.

26.

27.

28.

29.

30.

31.

32.

33.

34.

35.

36.

37.

38.

39.

40.

41.

42.

43.

44.

45.

46.

47.

48.

49.

50.

51.

52.

53.

54.

55.

Day: _____ of 5

Date:

Your Desired Manifestation:

1 .
2 .
3 .
4 .
5 .
6 .
7 .
8 .
9 .
10 .
11 .
12 .
13 .
14 .
15 .

16.

17.

18.

19.

20.

21.

22.

23.

24.

25.

26.

27.

28.

29.

30.

31.

32.

33.

34.

35.

36.

37.

38.

39.

40.

41.

42.

43.

44.

45.

46.

47.

48.

49.

50.

51.

52.

53.

54.

55.

Day: _____ of 5

Date:

Your Desired Manifestation:

_____

_____

_____

1 . _____

2 . _____

3 . _____

4 . _____

5 . _____

6 . _____

7 . _____

8 . _____

9 . _____

10 . _____

11 . _____

12 . _____

13 . _____

14 . _____

15 . _____

16 .

17 .

18 .

19 .

20.

21 .

22.

23.

24.

25.

26.

27.

28.

29.

30.

31 .

32.

33.

34.

35.

36.

37.

38.

39.

40.

41.

42.

43.

44.

45.

46.

47.

48.

49.

50.

51.

52.

53.

54.

55.

Day: _____ of 5

Date:

Your Desired Manifestation:

1 .
2 .
3 .
4 .
5 .
6 .
7 .
8 .
9 .
10 .
11 .
12 .
13 .
14 .
15 .

16 .

17 .

18 .

19 .

20.

21 .

22.

23 .

24.

25 .

26.

27 .

28.

29.

30.

31 .

32.

33 .

34.

35 .

36.

37.

38.

39.

40.

41.

42.

43.

44.

45.

46.

47.

48.

49.

50.

51.

52.

53.

54.

55.

Day: _____ of 5

Date:

Your Desired Manifestation:

1.
2.
3.
4.
5.
6.
7.
8.
9.
10.
11.
12.
13.
14.
15.

16.

17.

18.

19.

20.

21.

22.

23.

24.

25.

26.

27.

28.

29.

30.

31.

32.

33.

34.

35.

36.

37.

38.

39.

40.

41.

42.

43.

44.

45.

46.

47.

48.

49.

50.

51.

52.

53.

54.

55.

Day: _____ of 5

Date:

Your Desired Manifestation:

_____

_____

_____

1 . _____
2 . _____
3 . _____
4 . _____
5 . _____
6 . _____
7 . _____
8 . _____
9 . _____
10 . _____
11 . _____
12 . _____
13 . _____
14 . _____
15 . _____

16.

17.

18.

19.

20.

21.

22.

23.

24.

25.

26.

27.

28.

29.

30.

31.

32.

33.

34.

35.

36.

37.

38.

39.

40.

41.

42.

43.

44.

45.

46.

47.

48.

49.

50.

51.

52.

53.

54.

55.

Day: _____ of 5

Date:

Your Desired Manifestation:

1 .

2 .

3 .

4 .

5 .

6 .

7 .

8 .

9 .

10 .

11 .

12 .

13 .

14 .

15 .

16 .

17 .

18 .

19 .

20.

21 .

22 .

23 .

24 .

25 .

26 .

27 .

28 .

29 .

30.

31 .

32 .

33 .

34 .

35 .

36.

37.

38.

39.

40.

41.

42.

43.

44.

45.

46.

47.

48.

49.

50.

51.

52.

53.

54.

55.

CHAPTER 5

YOUR SCRIPTING MANIFESTATION SPACE

Date:

Your Desired Manifestation:

Date:

Your Desired Manifestation:

Date:

Your Desired Manifestation:

Date:

Your Desired Manifestation:

Date:

Your Desired Manifestation:

Date:

Your Desired Manifestation:

Date:

Your Desired Manifestation:

Date:

Your Desired Manifestation:

Date:

Your Desired Manifestation:

Date:

Your Desired Manifestation:

Law of Attraction Manifestation Journal

Date:

Your Desired Manifestation:

Date:

Your Desired Manifestation:

Date:

Your Desired Manifestation:

Date:

Your Desired Manifestation:

Date:

Your Desired Manifestation:

Date:

Your Desired Manifestation:

Date:

Your Desired Manifestation:

Date:

Your Desired Manifestation:

Date:

Your Desired Manifestation:

Date:

Your Desired Manifestation:

Date:

Your Desired Manifestation:

About the Author

LATHA JAY is a spiritual manifestation coach and Ayurvedic practitioner who blends modern knowledge with traditional wisdom. She integrates what she has learned through life experiences to teach people to shift perceptions, manifest, and live happier lives. She is passionate about guiding clients through lifestyle and mindset modifications to flat-out transform their lives with new experiences of happiness, freedom, and love.

When not working with clients, writing, spending time with her family, or building courses, Latha spends her days learning from others, farming, and persistently maintaining a beginner's mindset in everything. Learn more at LathaJay.com.